The Agile Workforce: Transforming Business with IT Staff Augmentation

Amola R. Mehta

Made with ❤ on the Notion Press Platform
www.notionpress.com

Over 14 Years of Transformation: A Passion for IT Staff Augmentation

Over the past 14 years, my career has evolved from a technical support role into a deep and abiding passion for IT staff augmentation. This journey has profoundly shaped both my professional and personal growth, fostering a deeper understanding of the intersection between people, technology, and organizational success. What began with a focus on systems and processes gradually transformed into a commitment to the human side of technology—helping businesses and individuals thrive together.

The Early Days: Building a Foundation in People and Technology

My career began as a Technical Support Executive, where I focused on resolving technical issues. However, it was the human connections I made during this time that left the deepest impact. This role taught me the value of empathy and communication—skills that later became instrumental in shaping my approach to IT staff augmentation.

The Role of Empathy: From Consultation to Recruitment

I later transitioned into roles that helped students and professionals navigate study and PR visa applications. While not directly tied to recruitment, these roles emphasized guiding individuals through critical life decisions. This experience heightened my emotional intelligence and reinforced the importance of understanding and addressing individual needs—an essential foundation for my future work in employee relations and talent management.

Discovering IT Staff Augmentation: People at the Core

It was during my time in the IT staff augmentation sector that I discovered my true passion. My role combined recruitment and employee relations, with a strong emphasis on the latter. I worked closely with both clients and candidates, ensuring not just the right hires but also their successful integration into organizational culture. It was here that I realized the true value of long-term relationships and fostering environments where employees and organizations could thrive.

Leadership and Balance: Growing as a Recruiter

As I advanced into leadership roles, managing accounts and teams, I learned that success in recruitment isn't just about meeting targets—it's about leading with empathy, creating balance, and building an atmosphere where both individuals and companies can achieve sustainable growth.

A Turning Point: A Strategic Approach to IT Staff Augmentation

A pivotal moment in my journey came when I fully embraced IT staff augmentation as a strategic driver of innovation and business growth. My role evolved from simply filling positions to solving complex organizational challenges and aligning talent with business needs.

I had the privilege of working under the mentorship of Nimit Bheda, whose guidance deeply influenced my approach. Nimit's vision underscored how recruitment could drive positive change for businesses and individuals alike, transforming challenges into opportunities.

Looking Ahead: Driving Growth and Connection

As the field of IT staff augmentation continues to evolve, I remain committed to my personal and professional growth. I aim to deepen relationships, foster innovation, and empower individuals to reach their full potential while helping businesses achieve their goals.

Defining the Journey: Passion for People and Growth

At the core of my career is a passion for people. From technical support to employee relations to IT staff augmentation, my focus has always been on understanding, connecting, and helping others succeed. Organizations thrive because of the people who drive them, and my mission has been to cultivate environments where both businesses and individuals can excel.

IT staff augmentation is more than recruitment—it's about finding the right people who align with a company's vision and culture. It's about building human connections that fuel growth and innovation. This is the world of IT staff augmentation, and my journey within it continues.

Contents

Introduction

What IT Staff Augmentation Is

In today's fast-moving and technology-driven business environment, companies are under constant pressure to innovate, stay competitive, and meet rapidly changing market demands. One of the key challenges businesses face is the need to scale their teams quickly and efficiently to address short-term project requirements, specialized skill gaps, or fluctuating workloads. This is where IT staff augmentation plays a crucial role.

IT staff augmentation is a strategic workforce model that enables organizations to temporarily integrate highly skilled IT professionals into their teams, often through third-party service providers. These professionals, typically experts in specific technologies or industries, work side-by-side with in-house teams to tackle specific tasks, fill skill gaps, and accelerate project timelines. Unlike outsourcing, where the vendor typically manages entire projects or functions independently, IT staff augmentation involves augmenting your internal team with specialized external resources that integrate seamlessly into your existing workflows.

For instance, imagine a financial services company embarking on a major digital transformation initiative, such as implementing a cloud-based enterprise resource planning (ERP) system. The company may already have a talented in-house IT team, but the specialized skills required for the cloud migration and system integration may be missing. Rather than hiring a full-time employee with cloud expertise—which would be costly and time-consuming—the company could leverage IT staff augmentation by partnering with a provider that can quickly deliver an experienced cloud architect, who can hit the ground running and contribute to the success of the project immediately. This approach provides the flexibility to meet specific project demands without the long-term commitment and expense of permanent hires.

The strength of IT staff augmentation lies in its flexibility. Businesses are no longer constrained by the limitations of traditional hiring practices, allowing them to scale their teams up or down according to project needs. Whether for a one-off project, seasonal increase in workload, or a specialized skill requirement, augmented teams provide the agility to meet fluctuating demands without the need to recruit, onboard, and train new full-time employees. Furthermore, these professionals are typically experts in their respective fields, allowing them to contribute value immediately, often with minimal onboarding time.

Purpose of the Book

This book aims to equip business leaders, IT managers, and HR professionals with the knowledge and strategies needed to effectively implement and manage IT staff augmentation. Whether you're looking to adopt staff augmentation for the first time or optimize an existing program, the insights and frameworks in this guide will help you navigate the complexities and opportunities associated with this staffing model.

The purpose of this book is twofold: first, to provide a deep understanding of what IT staff augmentation is and how it works, and second, to offer actionable guidance on how to implement, manage, and maximize its potential for your organization. You will learn how to assess your business needs, identify the right skills, select the right service provider, and integrate augmented professionals into your existing teams. Furthermore, this book delves into the specific challenges faced by both clients and service providers in the staff augmentation process, and offers solutions for overcoming those challenges.

By the end of this book, you will have a comprehensive understanding of how IT staff augmentation can help your business thrive. Whether your goal is to reduce hiring costs, access specialized expertise, or scale your workforce during peak demand periods, you'll be equipped with practical tools and strategies to leverage this powerful staffing model. Additionally, we will discuss the best practices for managing augmented teams, setting clear expectations, navigating contracts, and ensuring consistent project success.

Relevance in Today's IT Industry

The relevance of IT staff augmentation in today's business environment cannot be overstated. Technology is evolving at an unprecedented pace, with advancements in fields such as artificial intelligence (AI), cloud computing, cybersecurity, data science, and blockchain reshaping industries across the globe. For businesses to stay competitive, they must continually adopt new technologies, innovate their products and services, and address complex challenges.

However, this technological evolution comes with a significant challenge: the growing skills gap. According to the U.S. Bureau of Labor Statistics, there is an increasing shortage of qualified IT professionals, especially in high-demand fields such as AI development, cloud architecture, and cybersecurity. While businesses are investing heavily in digital transformation, they are often unable to find the necessary in-house talent to implement new technologies, leaving them struggling to keep pace with competitors.

For example, a large healthcare provider may wish to roll out a telemedicine platform using AI to enhance patient experience and streamline operations. To achieve this, they need AI engineers, cloud developers, and security experts who understand healthcare compliance standards. The traditional recruitment process may take months, and even then, the skills they need may not be readily available in their local market. This is where IT staff augmentation becomes a game-changer. By leveraging the global talent pool, the healthcare provider can quickly bring in experienced professionals from various geographies to build the platform, ensuring that the project stays on track and within budget.

Staff augmentation enables organizations to quickly access the talent they need without the prolonged hiring process or the overhead costs associated with full-time employees. Whether you are looking to implement a complex software solution, migrate your infrastructure to the cloud, or enhance your cybersecurity defenses, staff augmentation allows businesses to meet short-term, high-impact needs with precision.

Challenges and Solutions: While staff augmentation offers many benefits, it also comes with certain challenges that businesses and service providers must address to ensure success.

- Integration and Collaboration: One of the primary challenges clients face when integrating augmented professionals into their teams is ensuring smooth collaboration and alignment with in-house staff. Augmented professionals must quickly adapt to the company's culture, workflows, and communication systems. This can be particularly challenging when working across different time zones, languages, or organizational structures. To mitigate this, companies should establish clear onboarding processes, set expectations upfront, and use collaborative tools such as Slack, Trello, and Zoom to ensure continuous and transparent communication.
- Cultural and Operational Fit: From a service provider's perspective, ensuring that their professionals are not only technically proficient but also able to align with the client's culture and way of working is a significant challenge. This involves understanding not only the client's technical requirements but also their internal communication styles, decision-making processes, and team dynamics. Providers can overcome this challenge by conducting thorough pre-deployment assessments and offering training to ensure the augmented staff understands the client's specific operational nuances.
- Quality Control and Performance: Another challenge for both clients and providers is maintaining consistent quality control and managing the performance

of augmented staff. As augmented professionals are often brought in for short-term assignments, ensuring that they meet the client's high standards of quality, productivity, and innovation can be difficult. Service providers must establish clear performance metrics and offer ongoing support to ensure that the augmented professionals remain aligned with client expectations. Clients, on the other hand, must be proactive in setting clear KPIs and regularly reviewing the performance of augmented professionals to ensure that project milestones are met.

- The Remote Work Revolution: The rise of remote work has drastically changed the dynamics of IT staff augmentation. While it expands the talent pool by enabling companies to tap into global talent, it also brings challenges in terms of coordination, communication, and team integration. For service providers, managing remote teams requires careful attention to time zone differences, cultural diversity, and communication barriers. For clients, the key to success is adopting the right technology stack to facilitate seamless collaboration across borders, such as project management tools like Asana or Jira, as well as communication platforms like Microsoft Teams and Slack.
- Contractual and Legal Complexities: From both the client and service provider perspective, contractual agreements can present challenges. These agreements

must clearly define the roles, expectations, and responsibilities of all parties involved, especially when it comes to intellectual property, non-disclosure agreements, and confidentiality. Clients need to ensure that the contracts protect their business interests while giving them the flexibility they need. Service providers, in turn, must ensure that the contract is fair and provides adequate protection for their workers. Legal experts familiar with cross-border employment laws and IT-specific regulations must be involved to navigate these complexities.

As businesses continue to adapt to the demands of digital transformation, IT staff augmentation offers a critical solution to quickly scale teams, access specialized skills, and stay competitive. By addressing the challenges of integration, communication, and performance management, organizations can fully leverage the power of staff augmentation to accelerate their projects and meet the growing demands of the digital age.

In the chapters that follow, we will delve deeper into the benefits, best practices, and strategies for successful IT staff augmentation, helping you understand how to implement it effectively, manage augmented teams, and ultimately use it to drive business growth and innovation.

Chapter 1

Understanding the Core of IT Staff Augmentation

1.1 The Evolution of IT Staffing Models

The landscape of IT staffing has seen significant transformation over the past few decades, driven by shifts in technology, business needs, and workforce dynamics. Traditionally, organizations relied heavily on permanent, full-time employees who worked on-site. These employees were often expected to possess broad technical knowledge and undergo extensive onboarding processes. However, this approach was not without its challenges—long recruitment cycles, substantial administrative costs, and the inflexibility of hiring full-time staff for short-term or niche needs.

As the pace of technological innovation accelerated, businesses found themselves needing highly specialized talent—especially in areas like cloud computing, cybersecurity, data science, AI, and DevOps—at an unprecedented rate. The demand for such expertise, coupled with the growing shortage of skilled professionals, led to a reevaluation of traditional staffing models. Enter IT staff augmentation.

IT staff augmentation allows businesses to temporarily add specialized professionals to their in-house teams without the long-term commitment and cost of permanent hires. This model offers a more agile solution to fluctuating project demands. Unlike outsourcing, where an external vendor manages an entire project, augmented staff work directly within the company's existing structure. They integrate into teams, collaborate with internal staff, and provide expertise exactly where it is needed, from software development to cloud infrastructure management or machine learning model deployment.

This shift toward augmented staffing aligns with broader trends reshaping the workforce, including the rise of the gig economy, the increasing prevalence of remote work, and a growing emphasis on project-based work. IT staff augmentation is now a vital strategic tool that enables companies to adapt rapidly to change, bringing in the exact skills required for a limited time without committing to long-term financial or logistical burdens.

1.2 Key Benefits of IT Staff Augmentation

IT staff augmentation offers numerous advantages for both businesses and HR management. In a technology-driven world, the ability to scale your workforce quickly and effectively is a game-changer, and staff augmentation provides this flexibility in spades. Here are some of the primary benefits from both business and HR perspectives:

- Flexibility and Scalability

  In an era where projects evolve rapidly and business priorities can shift on short notice, the flexibility to scale your workforce quickly is essential. Staff augmentation allows businesses to bring in skilled professionals on demand, scaling up when project demands increase and scaling down when the work subsides. For example, a financial services firm may need specialized blockchain developers during a product launch but might not need them long-term after the project completes. IT staff augmentation fills this need perfectly.

- Cost Efficiency

  From a financial perspective, IT staff augmentation can be significantly more cost-effective than traditional hiring. Full-time employees entail long-term salary commitments, benefits packages, and training costs. With staff augmentation, companies only pay for the talent they need when they need it. This means that businesses can quickly manage project budgets and avoid unnecessary long-term expenses. Additionally, since augmented professionals bring their expertise with them, companies avoid the cost of investing in training programs for niche technologies like machine learning algorithms or advanced cloud architectures.

- Access to Specialized Talent

  As the IT landscape becomes more complex, businesses often find themselves in need of very specific technical expertise, such as data engineers, AI specialists, or cybersecurity experts with experience in handling emerging threats. Staff augmentation opens the door to a vast pool of highly skilled professionals who can hit the ground running. For example, a startup developing an IoT platform can quickly bring in cloud architects and embedded systems engineers to build and deploy the product—professionals with niche skills that are hard to find through traditional hiring channels.

- Quick Integration and Immediate Impact

  Augmented professionals are not just available on demand; they also come equipped with the experience to integrate quickly. Whether it's working with DevOps teams to streamline deployment pipelines or collaborating with data scientists to analyze large datasets, these professionals are experts in their respective fields and often need little ramp-up time. This allows businesses to maintain momentum on projects and meet critical deadlines, without having to invest time in lengthy training processes.

- Reduced Risk and Overhead

  IT staff augmentation reduces risks associated with permanent hiring. In a fast-paced environment, project needs can shift quickly. For instance, if a project encounters unforeseen challenges or pivots in a new direction, the business can adjust its workforce size without the burden of managing layoffs or employee retention. This ability to quickly scale staffing levels up or down gives businesses agility and ensures they are not overburdened with unnecessary overheads.

- Focus on Core Business Activities

  By augmenting their teams with external specialists, businesses can free up their internal staff to focus on core activities. For example, an enterprise-level e-commerce company might use augmented resources to enhance their backend systems with artificial intelligence-powered recommendation engines while their internal team continues to work on optimizing the customer experience and scaling the platform. This strategic delegation ensures that in-house teams can concentrate on their strengths while specialized experts handle their own areas.

1.3 Staff Augmentation vs. Traditional Outsourcing

While both staff augmentation and outsourcing are methods of utilizing external resources to fill skills gaps, there are distinct differences in how each approach works and the control a business retains.

- Project Control

  In traditional outsourcing, a company hands over an entire project to an external service provider, effectively relinquishing control over the processes, timelines, and deliverables. For instance, if a company outsources its cybersecurity function, the vendor manages the operations entirely, including staffing and compliance measures. Conversely, with IT staff augmentation, the company retains full control over the project. Augmented staff integrate into the internal team and work under the company's direction, ensuring that company processes, standards, and leadership are maintained throughout.

- Scope of Work

  Outsourcing is typically used for end-to-end project management. An organization might outsource a website redesign or the migration of infrastructure to the cloud, entrusting the service provider to handle everything. However, staff augmentation focuses on supplying professionals for specific, high-value roles. For example, a company may augment its team with a data scientist to improve its predictive analytics models, or it may bring in a cloud engineer to assist in a migration to AWS. In this case, the external professional works closely with the internal team, contributing directly to the project's success.

- Integration and Collaboration

  While outsourcing providers operate independently and may sometimes create barriers in communication or cultural integration, staff augmentation is all about collaboration. Augmented professionals work as part of the internal team, providing technical expertise while aligning with company objectives and culture. For example, a global software development firm might bring in augmented software engineers to work on specific features of a new product. These engineers collaborate closely with in-house product managers, designers, and developers, ensuring the project moves forward seamlessly.

1.4 Key Considerations for Implementing IT Staff Augmentation

Despite the many benefits of IT staff augmentation, its successful implementation requires careful planning and consideration from both business leaders and human resource managers. Here are key factors to ensure effective deployment:

- Understanding Business Needs

  Identifying the precise requirements of the project is the first step in leveraging staff augmentation effectively. This includes determining whether the need is for a short-term skill gap (e.g., a database administrator for a migration project) or for specialized expertise in a specific technology (e.g., cloud-native architecture). Clear objectives ensure that the right talent is sourced and that expectations are aligned from the outset.

- Selecting the Right Augmentation Partner

  Choosing the right provider is critical to the success of an augmentation strategy. HR managers and business leaders should partner with vendors that have a proven track record of supplying top-tier professionals. This means looking for firms with expertise in the relevant technological stacks—be it machine learning, blockchain, or data analytics—and a strong understanding of the company's industry needs. Compatibility with company culture and work processes should also be prioritized to ensure smooth integration.

- Clear Communication and Expectations

  A well-defined communication plan is essential. This includes setting expectations around the role, timeline, performance goals, and collaboration methods. For example, an e-commerce company working with augmented mobile developers must ensure alignment on product milestones, testing requirements, and collaboration tools to streamline communication.

- Integration with In-House Teams

  The success of IT staff augmentation hinges on effective collaboration between internal teams and augmented professionals. Proper onboarding, clear access to internal systems, and mutual respect between in-house employees and external staff are key to fostering a positive working environment and ensuring project success. HR should work closely with internal teams to create an integration plan that supports seamless collaboration.

- Managing Legal and Contractual Elements

  The legal framework for staff augmentation must be robust. Contracts should clearly define intellectual property ownership, non-disclosure agreements, performance expectations, and exit clauses. For example, if a company hires an augmented cloud security consultant for a specific project, it is essential that intellectual property rights are clearly outlined in the contract to protect both the company's and consultant's interests.

Chapter 2

The Key Benefits of IT Staff Augmentation

As the global business environment continues to evolve, characterized by rapid technological advancements, shifting market demands, and the need for organizational agility, businesses are under increasing pressure to innovate quickly while managing costs effectively. The traditional methods of hiring permanent staff or relying solely on outsourcing are often too rigid and slow to keep up with these demands. Enter IT staff augmentation—a strategic solution that allows businesses to remain competitive by rapidly adapting their workforce to meet specific project requirements. This model has become essential for businesses seeking to bridge skill gaps, accelerate project timelines, and maintain operational efficiency. In this chapter, we explore the critical benefits of IT staff augmentation and how it provides businesses with the flexibility, expertise, and speed necessary to thrive in the fast-paced world of modern IT.

2.1 Flexibility and Scalability

In today's unpredictable business landscape, flexibility and scalability are essential attributes for a workforce. Traditional staffing models often fail to provide the agility needed to respond quickly to changing project demands, market conditions, or new technological requirements. With long recruitment cycles and permanent hiring commitments, businesses may find themselves overstaffed during lean periods or understaffed when a surge in demand occurs.

IT staff augmentation solves this problem by offering a flexible solution where businesses can scale their workforce up or down based on the evolving needs of specific projects. For instance, a financial services firm rolling out a new cloud-based platform may need to temporarily expand its team with experts in cloud architecture, cybersecurity, and data engineering. With staff augmentation, the company can bring in highly specialized professionals with the right skill sets for a defined period, ensuring that the team is equipped to meet project deadlines without the burden of permanent staffing commitments.

This flexibility is particularly valuable when there's a need for specific technical expertise in emerging fields such as artificial intelligence (AI), machine learning, blockchain, or quantum computing. Businesses can quickly integrate experts in these areas into their existing teams to deliver on high-priority initiatives, all while avoiding the extensive time and cost investment of hiring full-time employees. For example, an e-commerce company looking to enhance its recommendation algorithms with machine learning can augment its data science team with specialized professionals who bring immediate value.

Additionally, IT staff augmentation enables companies to scale teams quickly without the long lead times typically associated with traditional recruitment. When a project reaches a new phase or an unexpected requirement arises, the company can quickly add the necessary skills and then scale back when those skills are no longer required. This on-demand scalability is critical for staying ahead in industries that are constantly changing.

2.2 Cost-Effectiveness

With tight budgets and the pressure to deliver results faster, businesses are increasingly turning to IT staff augmentation for its cost efficiency. The traditional process of hiring full-time employees often involves significant financial commitments—recruitment costs, salaries, benefits, onboarding, and training expenses. For businesses with fluctuating demands, this can lead to inefficiencies and overstaffing during slow periods.

In contrast, IT staff augmentation provides a cost-effective alternative. The financial model is project-based, which means companies only pay for the specific skills they need for the duration of the project. This model eliminates the need for long-term salary commitments and helps companies control costs more effectively. For example, an IT services firm working on a software upgrade project may only need specific expertise in cybersecurity for the initial phase. Rather than hiring a full-time cybersecurity expert, the firm can engage an augmented professional for a few months, ensuring that its budget remains aligned with the project's needs.

Furthermore, by avoiding the overhead of hiring permanent staff and reducing training costs, businesses can allocate more resources toward core business activities. Augmented professionals bring pre-existing expertise, reducing the time spent on ramp-up and training. For example, a global retailer seeking to implement a new CRM platform can quickly integrate a Salesforce expert into its team through staff augmentation, saving both time and money by bypassing the hiring and training process.

2.3 Access to Specialized Talent

As technology continues to advance, the demand for specialized talent in areas such as cloud computing, data analytics, cybersecurity, AI, and blockchain has surged. However, the shortage of qualified professionals in these fields has created significant challenges for businesses trying to fill skill gaps.

IT staff augmentation offers businesses immediate access to a global pool of highly skilled professionals who possess deep expertise in niche technologies. Whether it's implementing a multi-cloud infrastructure, enhancing machine learning algorithms, or ensuring robust security practices, augmented professionals can provide the specialized knowledge necessary to tackle complex challenges. For example, a financial institution looking to implement a secure blockchain-based transaction system can augment its team with a blockchain developer who already has hands-on experience with the latest protocols, ensuring that the project is executed with precision and expertise.

Moreover, augmented staff are often more adaptable than permanent hires because they come with a wealth of experience across different industries and technological stacks. This versatility enables them to adapt quickly to new challenges, contributing to multiple aspects of a project. For instance, a healthcare organization needing expertise in both cloud migration and HIPAA-compliant data security can engage a professional who is proficient in both areas, without having to hire two separate full-time employees.

The global reach of IT staff augmentation also allows businesses to tap into talent that may not be locally available, thus overcoming geographic constraints. With remote work becoming more common, companies can hire professionals from anywhere in the world, ensuring access to the best talent without being limited by location.

2.4 Speed of Deployment

Time-to-market is a critical factor for many businesses, particularly in industries like tech, finance, and healthcare, where rapid innovation is a competitive advantage. IT staff augmentation accelerates project timelines by enabling businesses to quickly assemble and deploy teams of skilled professionals who can integrate seamlessly into existing workflows.

Unlike traditional recruitment, which involves lengthy advertising, interviewing, and onboarding processes, IT staff augmentation allows businesses to tap into a ready pool of talent. Augmented staff are typically already familiar with the technologies and methodologies required for the project, meaning they can start contributing almost immediately. For example, a software development company working on a product release can rapidly augment its team with front-end developers experienced in React, ensuring that the user interface is completed on schedule without delays.

This speed of deployment is particularly beneficial when companies face tight deadlines or sudden shifts in project requirements. For example, when a cloud infrastructure failure disrupts operations, an augmented DevOps engineer can be deployed quickly to restore services, minimizing downtime and ensuring business continuity. Similarly, when a tech startup needs to release a beta version of its app ahead of competitors, augmented UI/UX designers can be brought on to ensure that the interface meets high standards without sacrificing the timeline.

2.5 Risk Mitigation

IT staff augmentation helps mitigate several risks that businesses face with traditional hiring methods. Hiring the wrong candidate can be costly and time-consuming, and businesses may struggle with underperforming employees, poor cultural fit, or a mismatch between skills and project needs. IT staff augmentation reduces these risks by offering a flexible, performance-based model that allows businesses to evaluate augmented professionals on a short-term basis before making longer-term commitments.

For example, if a project changes direction, companies can easily adjust the team size and composition without being locked into long-term obligations. Additionally, because augmented professionals are often highly experienced, the risk of poor performance is minimized. These professionals are experts in their field and can contribute effectively from day one, which reduces the likelihood of project delays or quality issues.

Moreover, working with staffing agencies helps mitigate administrative and legal risks. The service provider handles aspects like tax compliance, labor laws, and intellectual property agreements, allowing businesses to focus on project execution. This is particularly important in industries with strict regulatory requirements, such as healthcare and finance, where compliance is critical.

Conclusion

The benefits of IT staff augmentation are clear: it provides businesses with the flexibility, cost-efficiency, specialized talent, and rapid deployment needed to stay competitive in a fast-evolving market. However, successfully leveraging staff augmentation requires careful planning, clear communication, and a strategic partnership with a trusted staffing provider. For businesses looking to remain agile, enhance innovation, and scale effectively, IT staff augmentation offers an invaluable solution that meets the dynamic needs of today's technological landscape.

Chapter 3

Challenges in IT Staff Augmentation

While IT staff augmentation offers businesses considerable benefits, it also comes with a set of challenges that, if not properly addressed, can undermine the effectiveness of this staffing model. These challenges stem from the complexities of managing remote, temporary, and specialized talent while ensuring that external professionals are seamlessly integrated into existing internal teams. Effective communication, collaboration, cultural alignment, and maintaining quality control are all crucial to the success of staff augmentation initiatives. In this chapter, we examine the key challenges businesses face when implementing IT staff augmentation, and offer strategies to mitigate these challenges from both the client and service provider perspectives.

3.1 Communication and Collaboration Across Teams

Effective communication is critical to the success of any project, but it becomes particularly challenging when teams are composed of both internal employees and external augmented staff. One of the biggest barriers to communication arises from differences in work styles, communication tools, and practices. Internal teams may be accustomed to collaborating via platforms like Slack, Microsoft Teams, or Zoom, while augmented staff might prefer email, project management tools like Jira, or other communication channels. These differences can lead to breakdowns in communication, missed messages, and delays in project timelines.

For example, a software development team working on a multi-phase cloud migration project may consist of both internal developers and augmented cloud specialists. If the augmented professionals are accustomed to a different project management software or communication frequency, key updates may be overlooked or delayed, ultimately affecting the project's success.

Additionally, remote work arrangements—often a hallmark of IT staff augmentation—can amplify communication gaps. With virtual interactions, subtle nuances may be lost, and important conversations can be missed, leading to misalignments and inefficiencies. For instance, when working across time zones or in asynchronous environments, a team in the U.S. might send a project update overnight that isn't read by the augmented team in Europe until the next working day. This delay can cause cascading project delays.

Solution: To mitigate these communication challenges, businesses must establish clear communication protocols at the outset of the project. This includes defining the preferred communication channels, response times, and meeting cadences. For instance, setting up daily stand-up meetings via video calls, weekly status updates, and using a shared project management platform like Asana or Trello can ensure everyone stays on the same page. Additionally, fostering a culture of open communication, where augmented staff are encouraged to ask questions and provide feedback, can improve transparency and trust between the teams.

3.2 Integrating Augmented Staff with Existing Teams

Successful integration of augmented staff with in-house teams is another significant challenge in IT staff augmentation. While external professionals are hired for their specialized expertise, ensuring they blend effectively with the internal team's culture, workflows, and objectives requires careful planning. If integration is not handled well, it can lead to friction, misunderstandings, and inefficiencies.

For example, imagine a marketing team working with an augmented data scientist to enhance its customer analytics capabilities. If the data scientist does not understand the team's existing processes or the company's brand tone, their contributions might not align with the internal team's goals. This could result in deliverables that don't meet expectations, causing delays and frustration.

The integration challenge also includes aligning roles and responsibilities between internal employees and augmented staff. Without clear delineation of duties, confusion and overlap can occur. For instance, if both an internal project manager and an augmented IT architect are overseeing the same component of a software deployment without clear role definitions, the project may experience redundancy or lack direction.

Solution: A structured onboarding process is essential for smooth integration. Augmented staff should be introduced to the company's culture, values, tools, workflows, and expectations. A formal orientation program, where augmented professionals are familiarized with internal procedures and communication styles, can facilitate a more seamless transition. Moreover, internal teams should collaborate with augmented staff to establish clear roles and responsibilities from the outset. Defining these roles helps eliminate ambiguity, reduces overlap, and promotes a sense of shared ownership of the project's success.

3.3 Cultural and Timezone Differences

In the globalized world of IT staff augmentation, cultural and timezone differences can present significant challenges, especially when working with remote teams. While these differences provide access to a broader talent pool, they can also lead to misunderstandings and friction if not managed appropriately.

Cultural differences—ranging from communication styles to work ethics—can affect how teams collaborate. For example, in some cultures, team members may be expected to provide direct, candid feedback, while in others, communication may be more indirect or reserved. Misalignments in these styles can result in tension, confusion, or missed opportunities for collaboration. Similarly, different attitudes towards hierarchy, decision-making, and problem-solving approaches can further complicate the working relationship.

Additionally, when staff augmentation involves working with teams across different time zones, the challenge of synchronizing meetings and collaboration becomes even more pronounced. For example, a software company with internal staff in New York and augmented developers in India might face difficulties in aligning working hours for collaborative efforts. This often leads to delays in communication, missed meetings, and additional effort to manage asynchronous work.

Solution: To overcome cultural challenges, businesses should foster cultural sensitivity by providing cross-cultural training for both internal and augmented teams. This training can help team members understand and respect different communication styles, work ethics, and decision-making processes. Furthermore, businesses should encourage an open dialogue about cultural differences, allowing teams to express concerns and adapt to each other's approaches.

Timezone differences can be mitigated by establishing flexible working hours and identifying core overlapping hours where both internal and augmented teams can collaborate in real-time. Additionally, utilizing asynchronous communication tools, such as recorded video updates or a shared project management system, ensures that the project continues to progress even when real-time collaboration is not possible.

3.4 Maintaining Quality Control and Consistency

Maintaining consistent quality control when working with augmented staff is one of the most challenging aspects of IT staff augmentation. Since augmented professionals are external, businesses may find it difficult to ensure that their work aligns with internal quality standards, coding practices, and overall project goals. This challenge can be exacerbated when external staff join at various stages of a project, or when there is a high degree of technical complexity.

For example, consider a company that brings in augmented software engineers to work on different modules of a large-scale enterprise resource planning (ERP) system. If these engineers use different coding conventions or testing methodologies, it can lead to inconsistencies that affect the overall quality of the project. Inconsistent documentation standards and variations in technical approaches can also create problems during system integration, making it difficult for internal teams to maintain continuity and deliver a polished final product.

Solution: To ensure quality control and consistency, businesses should establish clear quality benchmarks and guidelines at the outset of the project. Internal teams should work closely with augmented staff to communicate expectations regarding coding standards, testing protocols, and documentation practices. Setting up regular code reviews and incorporating automated testing tools can help catch discrepancies early. Additionally, appointing internal team members to oversee quality assurance can ensure that the augmented staff's work meets company standards.

Maintaining an open feedback loop between internal and augmented staff is crucial. Regular check-ins, coupled with real-time collaboration, can help identify potential issues and make adjustments as needed. If necessary, businesses can also offer ongoing training to augmented staff, helping them stay up to date on internal processes, tools, and practices.

Conclusion

While IT staff augmentation provides businesses with access to specialized talent, faster project deployment, and improved scalability, it also presents several challenges that require careful management. Effective communication, seamless integration with internal teams, cultural and timezone alignment, and maintaining high-quality standards are all critical factors that can influence the success of an augmentation strategy. By addressing these challenges proactively—through structured onboarding, clear role definition, cross-cultural training, and continuous quality oversight—businesses can ensure that their augmented teams operate efficiently, collaborate effectively, and contribute meaningfully to the success of IT projects. For both clients and service providers, focusing on these key areas is essential to maximizing the value of staff augmentation and achieving long-term project success.

Chapter 4

Strategies for Overcoming Challenges in IT Staff Augmentation

IT staff augmentation offers businesses access to specialized expertise and scalability, allowing them to tap into a broader talent pool. However, realizing the full potential of this staffing model requires careful management and strategic planning to overcome challenges such as communication gaps, integration issues, cultural and timezone differences, and maintaining consistent quality. From both a business and human resource management perspective, addressing these challenges proactively ensures that augmented teams seamlessly integrate with internal operations, driving greater success. In this chapter, we will explore actionable strategies to overcome these obstacles, supported by case studies, research-backed insights, and real-world examples.

4.1 Communication and Collaboration Across Teams

Effective communication lies at the heart of successful IT staff augmentation. Whether teams are co-located or dispersed across different regions, clear and consistent communication is essential to meeting project objectives on time and with the desired quality. Communication barriers can result in missed deadlines, confusion over roles, and reduced morale among team members.

Strategic Approach:

- Establish Clear Communication Protocols: From the outset, ensure all team members are aligned on communication preferences and expectations. Define the tools to be used for day-to-day communication—whether it's Slack, Microsoft Teams, or Zoom for meetings—and set clear guidelines for response times. For example, internal teams might prefer quick check-ins via Slack, while augmented developers might rely more on project management tools like Jira for tracking progress and handling issues. Clear expectations prevent miscommunication and streamline workflows across disparate teams.
- Schedule Regular Touchpoints: Augmented teams, particularly those working remotely or in different

time zones, can sometimes feel disconnected from the core team. Regular touchpoints such as daily stand-ups, weekly sprint reviews, and occasional brainstorming sessions help maintain engagement, align priorities, and ensure everyone is on the same page. These touchpoints foster an ongoing feedback loop, crucial for both internal and augmented staff to thrive and address issues in real-time.

- Leverage Project Management Tools: Tools like Jira, Trello, Asana, or Monday.com can bridge the communication gap by providing transparency into individual progress and facilitating seamless collaboration. These tools enable teams to track tasks, visualize workflows, and keep everyone aligned on project goals, regardless of their location. For instance, when managing an Agile development project, these platforms allow augmented developers to log progress and blockers, which internal teams can review and address in real-time.
- Real-Life Example: A global software company working on a cloud infrastructure project faced communication breakdowns when it added augmented cloud architects and engineers from multiple regions. By implementing daily video stand-ups and using Jira to manage tasks and progress, the teams overcame communication barriers. The result was improved collaboration, clearer responsibilities, and an on-time delivery with enhanced quality control.

4.2 Integrating Augmented Staff with Existing Teams

While the technical expertise of augmented staff is a clear advantage, integrating them with internal teams can be challenging. Misalignment in team culture, workflow practices, or role responsibilities can lead to inefficiencies and missed deadlines, making integration a critical factor for success.

Strategic Approach:

- Structured Onboarding Process: A well-structured onboarding program is essential for helping augmented staff seamlessly integrate into existing teams. This process should cover not just technical aspects, but also an introduction to the company's culture, values, and internal processes. Assigning a mentor or team liaison can further help new team members adjust. For instance, an augmented database specialist working with a business intelligence team should receive training on internal database standards, reporting tools (like Tableau or Power BI), and the company's data governance policies to ensure consistency.
- Role Clarity and Task Allocation: To minimize ambiguity, clearly define roles and responsibilities for both internal and augmented staff. This will ensure that each team member understands how their contributions fit into the broader project. For

example, if internal project managers are handling client communications and augmented developers are focused on backend architecture, assigning clear tasks based on expertise avoids duplication and improves efficiency.

- Promote a Collaborative, Team-Oriented Culture: Foster a sense of inclusivity and ownership among augmented staff. While they may initially join on a temporary basis, treating them as full members of the team helps build trust and collaboration. For instance, including augmented staff in team-wide planning sessions, encouraging them to participate in internal workshops, and providing opportunities for professional development helps to build a stronger, more cohesive team.
- Case Study: A multinational e-commerce company brought in augmented IT professionals for a large-scale digital transformation. Initial role ambiguity led to project delays, but after implementing structured onboarding and hosting cross-functional workshops, the augmented staff integrated smoothly with the internal team. As a result, the company saw significant improvements in project delivery timelines, collaboration, and overall quality of the transformation process.

4.3 Navigating Cultural and Timezone Differences

IT staff augmentation often brings together teams from different cultural backgrounds and time zones, creating both opportunities for innovation and challenges in communication. While these differences can lead to creative problem-solving, they can also result in misunderstandings and logistical hurdles if not managed properly.

Strategic Approach:

- Foster Cultural Awareness and Sensitivity: Provide cultural training to both internal and augmented teams. Understanding diverse communication styles, decision-making approaches, and work ethics can minimize friction. For example, team members from hierarchical cultures may expect clear directives from leadership, whereas those from more egalitarian cultures may value collaborative decision-making. By understanding these differences, teams can interact more effectively, reducing the risk of miscommunication or frustration.
- Synchronize Timezones: Timezone differences can be one of the biggest challenges in staff augmentation. However, by establishing core overlapping hours for collaboration, teams can ensure synchronous communication and decision-making. For example, a team based in New York and augmented staff in Bangalore can schedule a few hours in the morning for

real-time discussions, while leveraging asynchronous tools for updates outside of this window.

- Flexible Work Schedules: When working with teams spread across multiple time zones, offering flexible work schedules can help improve productivity. Flexible hours allow teams to work at times that suit their individual schedules, while still ensuring collaboration during key overlapping hours. Research from Global Workplace Analytics suggests that offering flexible work arrangements can boost productivity by 25%, particularly in remote work settings.
- Research Insight: A global consulting firm implemented flexible working hours across its augmented teams in different time zones. By accommodating different schedules and establishing dedicated overlapping hours, the firm was able to maintain continuous progress on client projects, while ensuring that real-time collaboration occurred when it mattered most.

4.4 Ensuring Consistent Quality Control

Maintaining consistent quality across augmented teams is crucial to ensure the integrity of the final product. The challenge lies in aligning the work of external professionals with internal standards and best practices, particularly when specialized skills or complex technologies are involved.

Strategic Approach:

- Set Clear Quality Benchmarks: At the project's inception, define clear quality standards that both internal and augmented staff must adhere to. This includes coding standards, documentation formats, testing protocols, and any other relevant benchmarks. For example, if augmented developers are working on a cloud-based application using AWS or Azure, they should be briefed on internal cloud security protocols, architecture standards, and testing frameworks to ensure consistency with company practices.
- Continuous Monitoring and Feedback: Regular reviews and feedback sessions throughout the project lifecycle help maintain quality control. Assign internal team members, such as QA specialists, to monitor augmented staff output and provide ongoing feedback. This ensures that deliverables meet quality standards and helps identify any issues early in the process.
- Standardized Tools and Practices: To ensure uniformity, establish a standardized toolset for both internal and augmented teams. Whether it's using GitHub for version control, Jenkins for continuous integration, or automated testing frameworks like Selenium or TestComplete, having a consistent set of tools ensures that workflows are standardized across teams, facilitating smoother collaboration and integration of their work.

- Real-Life Example: A global financial services company tasked augmented IT professionals with migrating its core banking systems. The initial work suffered from inconsistencies in code quality and documentation. By introducing a dedicated internal QA team to oversee the work and providing augmented staff with training on company-specific development practices, the company was able to ensure that external contributions aligned with internal standards. This led to improved quality, faster delivery, and a seamless migration.

Conclusion

While IT staff augmentation offers businesses the flexibility to scale rapidly and access specialized skills, overcoming the challenges it presents requires more than just technical expertise. By implementing strategic approaches to communication, integration, cultural sensitivity, and quality control, businesses can ensure that augmented teams seamlessly integrate with internal operations and contribute meaningfully to project success.

For both clients and service providers, fostering collaboration, aligning expectations, and continuously monitoring progress are essential to realizing the full potential of staff augmentation and achieving long-term business success.

Chapter 5

Key Roles in IT Staff Augmentation

In the modern business landscape, IT staff augmentation offers companies an invaluable resource to enhance capabilities, innovate, and accelerate project delivery. With digital transformation becoming a top priority for organizations, the need for skilled IT professionals has never been greater. Through IT staff augmentation, businesses can access top-tier talent and specialized skills without the long-term commitment of hiring full-time employees. However, to leverage the full potential of this staffing model, it's essential to understand the various roles that are commonly augmented and how they can influence project outcomes. This chapter will explore these key roles, discuss the challenges from both client and service provider perspectives, and highlight practical examples of how augmented professionals contribute to business success.

5.1 Commonly Augmented IT Roles

- Software Developers

  Software developers are one of the most frequently augmented roles, critical for building, maintaining, and enhancing software applications, whether for web, mobile, or desktop platforms. As technology evolves at a rapid pace, businesses often need additional development resources for specific initiatives, such as software upgrades, new product features, or scalability improvements.

Key Skills:

- Proficiency in programming languages such as Java, Python, JavaScript, C++, or C#
- Familiarity with front-end (React, Angular) or back-end (Node.js, Spring Boot) technologies
- Experience with Agile, Scrum, or DevOps methodologies
- Knowledge of cloud platforms (AWS, Azure, Google Cloud)

Case Study: A leading global e-commerce platform faced a challenge when they needed to roll out a major mobile app update. Their in-house development team was already at full capacity managing other projects. They decided to augment their team with mobile developers skilled in React Native and iOS development. The augmented team worked closely with the in-house team, ensuring seamless integration into the existing project timeline. This strategic augmentation allowed the company to launch the update ahead of schedule, improving user experience and customer retention.

- Data Scientists and Data Engineers

  Data scientists and data engineers play a pivotal role in transforming raw data into actionable insights, particularly as businesses strive to harness the power of big data, machine learning, and artificial intelligence (AI) for decision-making and strategic advantage. Augmenting teams with these experts enables companies to make data-driven decisions with precision.

Key Skills:

- Expertise in statistical analysis, machine learning algorithms, and data modeling
- Proficiency with programming languages such as Python, R, SQL, and familiarity with big data tools like Hadoop, Spark, and Apache Kafka
- Experience in data visualization tools like Tableau or Power BI
- Knowledge of cloud-based data storage and processing solutions

Case Study: A financial services firm sought to enhance its predictive analytics for risk assessment but lacked in-house expertise in machine learning. They augmented their team with a senior data scientist and a data engineer skilled in AI and machine learning technologies. The augmented team quickly developed a predictive model that improved the firm's risk assessment capabilities, leading to better decision-making, reduced operational risk, and a competitive edge in the market.

- Network Engineers

  Network engineers are vital to building and maintaining the infrastructure that supports secure and scalable business operations, especially as companies increasingly adopt cloud-based services and support remote workforces. Network engineers ensure that an organization's network is resilient, secure, and capable of handling growing demands.

Key Skills:

- Expertise in networking protocols (TCP/IP, DNS, DHCP) and network design
- Knowledge of firewall configuration, VPNs, and intrusion detection systems
- Experience with cloud network services (AWS VPC, Azure Networking)
- Familiarity with network monitoring tools (SolarWinds, Nagios)

Case Study: A multinational corporation with an expanding remote workforce needed to overhaul its network security to accommodate the growing number of off-site employees. The company augmented its team with a cloud security specialist who implemented a robust, secure, and scalable network architecture. This expert introduced secure VPN solutions and re-engineered the company's cloud infrastructure, reducing network breaches by 40% and enabling continued global expansion without compromising security.

- Cloud Architects and Cloud Engineers

  The shift to cloud computing has made cloud architects and engineers indispensable. These professionals design and implement cloud solutions that enable scalable, flexible, and cost-effective services for modern businesses.

Key Skills:

- Expertise in leading cloud platforms like AWS, Microsoft Azure, and Google Cloud
- Proficiency with containerization technologies (Docker, Kubernetes) and Infrastructure as Code (Terraform, Ansible)
- Deep understanding of cloud security and best practices in compliance
- Knowledge of cloud-native applications and services

Case Study: A healthcare provider required assistance to migrate its on-premise infrastructure to the cloud to meet regulatory standards and improve system scalability. They augmented their IT team with a cloud architect and cloud engineers who worked together to ensure a seamless migration. The cloud solution implemented not only met compliance and security standards but also reduced IT infrastructure costs by 30%, improving system reliability and ensuring continued regulatory adherence.

- Cybersecurity Specialists

  With the increasing frequency and sophistication of cyberattacks, organizations face constant threats to their systems, data, and operations. Cybersecurity specialists help businesses safeguard their digital assets and ensure compliance with data protection regulations.

Key Skills:

- Expertise in penetration testing, vulnerability management, and threat hunting
- Knowledge of firewalls, encryption techniques, and security protocols
- Experience with industry compliance standards (e.g., GDPR, HIPAA, PCI-DSS)
- Familiarity with cybersecurity tools such as Splunk, Wireshark, and Metasploit

Case Study: A global tech company was targeted by several cyberattacks that compromised sensitive customer data. In response, they augmented their team with a group of ethical hackers and cybersecurity specialists to conduct a security audit and vulnerability assessment. The augmented team identified critical security gaps and recommended solutions that led to a 50% reduction in breaches, improving both the company's reputation and customer trust.

5.2 The Impact of Augmented IT Professionals on Project Success

IT staff augmentation offers organizations the opportunity to bridge skill gaps and access specialized knowledge as needed. These professionals are critical to overcoming technical challenges, ensuring that projects are completed on time, within scope, and with the desired quality.

Key Success Factors:

- Access to Expertise: Augmented professionals bring in-depth, specialized skills that complement the capabilities of existing in-house teams. Whether it's building an app, implementing a machine learning model, or securing infrastructure, these experts provide the knowledge required to tackle specific challenges.

- Flexibility and Scalability: IT staff augmentation allows businesses to scale their teams rapidly based on project needs. This flexibility is invaluable when companies need to address short-term projects or fluctuating workloads without the commitment of full-time hires.
- Cost Efficiency: By tapping into a pool of experienced professionals only when required, businesses can avoid the overhead costs of permanent hires while still accessing top talent. This results in cost savings, especially when augmenting teams for short-term projects or for specific expertise.

5.3 Conclusion

IT staff augmentation is a powerful tool for businesses seeking to overcome skill shortages and accelerate the delivery of their projects. Whether businesses require developers to write software, data scientists to analyze big data, or cybersecurity specialists to protect valuable assets, augmenting internal teams with the right professionals can drive success. By selecting roles that are specifically suited to project needs, companies can fill gaps in expertise, ensure that projects stay on track, and remain competitive in an increasingly digital world.

By providing real-world examples and discussing challenges from both the client and service provider perspectives, we have seen how IT staff augmentation can be an essential strategy for companies to access the specialized skills they need, deliver quality outcomes, and successfully navigate the evolving technological landscape.

Chapter 6

Best Practices for Managing Augmented Teams

As businesses increasingly leverage IT staff augmentation to access specialized expertise, successfully managing augmented teams requires more than just technical acumen. It requires robust leadership, effective project management practices, and the ability to cultivate an inclusive, collaborative work environment where both internal and augmented staff can thrive. From a business and human resource management perspective, the key to success lies in how organizations integrate external professionals into their existing teams, ensure clear communication, and foster a sense of belonging—whether they are in-house employees or remote augmented specialists.

In this chapter, we will discuss best practices for managing augmented IT teams, emphasizing leadership, communication, and team integration. We'll explore how companies can overcome challenges that arise from remote working, different time zones, and diverse cultural backgrounds, while maximizing the potential of augmented staff to drive business outcomes.

6.1 Leadership and Project Management for Augmented Teams

Leadership and strong project management are the foundation of successful augmented teams, particularly when the team members are geographically dispersed or come from different organizational cultures. It is essential to establish clear goals, maintain consistent leadership, and foster a culture of accountability and collaboration. Effective project management ensures that both internal and augmented staff are aligned with the company's objectives and can contribute toward achieving project milestones.

Strategic Approach

- Set Clear Expectations and Align Goals: From day one, it's crucial to set clear expectations for all team members, both internal and augmented. The project's goals, timelines, and individual responsibilities should be communicated transparently. Employing methodologies like SMART (Specific, Measurable, Achievable, Relevant, Time-bound) goals can help set clear and realistic benchmarks, ensuring everyone is working towards the same objectives.

Example: A leading healthcare provider augmented its internal IT team with external software developers for a time-sensitive electronic health records (EHR) system update. By establishing clear deadlines, project scope, and deliverables from the start, they ensured smooth collaboration. As a result, the project was delivered on time, improving system usability and patient data management.

- Consistent Leadership and Guidance: A dedicated team lead or project manager should be assigned to oversee the augmented team. This leader should ensure seamless integration with the internal team and clarify expectations around workflows, deliverables, and the overall strategic direction of the project.

  Example: A fintech company brought in cloud engineers for a critical system migration. By assigning an experienced internal project manager to guide the augmented engineers, the project was kept on track, ensuring that the new infrastructure met security and compliance standards without delays.

- Accountability and Performance Monitoring: Encouraging a culture of accountability within augmented teams is vital. Both internal and external team members should take ownership of their roles and be held responsible for their deliverables. Regular check-ins, progress reports, and feedback sessions help track performance and address potential issues before they escalate.

Example: An international e-commerce company augmented its team with data scientists to implement advanced machine learning algorithms. Regular sprint reviews and data-driven KPIs helped keep the augmented staff aligned with internal teams, leading to the successful implementation of personalized product recommendations that drove a 20% increase in sales.

6.2 Building Strong Communication Channels

Communication remains one of the most significant challenges when managing augmented teams, especially with remote and offshore workers. Geographic distances, cultural differences, and varying time zones can introduce complexities in ensuring that all team members are aligned and updated. However, effective communication is essential for the success of any IT project, particularly when augmented teams are involved.

Strategic Approach

- Invest in the Right Communication Tools: The tools used for communication can significantly impact a team's effectiveness. Tools like Slack for messaging, Zoom or Microsoft Teams for virtual meetings, and Jira, Trello, or Asana for project management can facilitate real-time updates, keep tasks organized, and foster collaboration between internal and augmented staff. The right combination of tools ensures that both synchronous and asynchronous communication flows seamlessly, regardless of team members' locations.

Example: A software development company integrated augmented front-end and back-end developers using Slack for day-to-day communication, Jira for task management, and Zoom for weekly sprint meetings. This combination ensured alignment across their global teams and helped avoid delays in project timelines.

- Develop a Unified Communication Strategy: To address time zone and geographical differences, establish clear guidelines for communication, ensuring team members know when to expect responses and the preferred channels for various types of communication. For example, urgent matters can be addressed through a live meeting or phone call, while less time-sensitive issues may be handled via email or task management tools.

  Example: A global consulting firm faced challenges with asynchronous communication when augmenting their IT team for a complex cloud implementation. They implemented daily stand-up calls at overlapping hours for different time zones, supplemented by Slack channels for quick queries and updates. This communication strategy ensured efficient collaboration and timely problem resolution, reducing the risk of delays.

- Encourage Open Dialogue and Transparency: Transparency is key to building trust within augmented teams. Open and honest communication, where team members feel comfortable sharing concerns, ideas, and feedback, fosters a positive work environment. Both internal employees and augmented staff should be encouraged to speak up and voice their thoughts, ensuring issues are addressed proactively.

  Example: A multinational telecom company that augmented its IT department with network engineers for a complex infrastructure overhaul emphasized open dialogue across teams. Through Slack channels dedicated to knowledge-sharing and weekly all-hands calls, team members from different locations could ask questions, clarify doubts, and exchange best practices, leading to smoother project execution.

6.3 Integrating Remote Workers and Fostering a Unified Team

Managing remote augmented workers presents unique challenges, primarily related to team integration and engagement. Remote workers may feel disconnected from the company's culture or struggle with feelings of isolation. It's essential to proactively foster a cohesive team environment, regardless of physical distance.

Strategic Approach

- Effective Onboarding for Augmented Staff: The onboarding process should go beyond technical training—it should include introducing augmented staff to the company's culture, values, and internal processes. A well-structured onboarding program builds rapport and aligns external team members with internal standards. Assigning a mentor or a point person within the team can provide the support needed to integrate smoothly.

  Example: An AI-driven healthcare startup integrated augmented machine learning engineers by designing a comprehensive onboarding process that included a virtual company tour, introductions to key team members, and training on internal collaboration tools. This fostered a sense of belonging and ensured a smoother integration process.

- Promote Virtual Team Bonding: Virtual team-building activities are essential for cultivating relationships among remote team members. Whether it's a casual virtual coffee break, collaborative brainstorming session, or team quiz, these activities can help break down barriers, improve communication, and foster collaboration across geographical boundaries.

  Example: A SaaS company with an augmented customer success team in multiple countries organized virtual escape rooms and online hackathons, allowing augmented and in-house team members to connect on a personal level. This improved team dynamics and enhanced collaboration, especially when dealing with customer service and technical queries.

- Encourage Cross-Cultural Awareness: In global teams, understanding and respecting cultural differences is crucial. By promoting cultural awareness, companies can avoid misunderstandings and enhance teamwork. This includes training on how to communicate across cultures, addressing potential language barriers, and acknowledging diverse working styles.

  Example: A technology services company that augmented its IT team with developers from Eastern Europe and Asia implemented cross-cultural training sessions. These sessions educated the team on communication preferences and work habits across regions, leading to more respectful and effective collaboration.

6.4 Conclusion

Effectively managing augmented IT teams requires a strategic and holistic approach. By combining clear leadership, strong communication, and intentional team integration, businesses can maximize the potential of augmented staff and ensure successful project outcomes. Whether through aligning goals from the start, investing in the right communication tools, or fostering an inclusive team environment, organizations can overcome the challenges that come with augmenting their workforce and unlock new levels of productivity and innovation.

As we move into the next chapter, we will explore how organizations can track and evaluate the performance of augmented teams to ensure continuous improvement and optimize their IT staff augmentation strategies for the future.

Chapter 7

Emerging Trends and the Future of IT Staff Augmentation

The IT staff augmentation landscape is rapidly evolving, driven by advances in technology, changing workforce dynamics, and the increasing need for specialized skills. As companies seek to scale their IT capabilities through flexible, on-demand talent, staying ahead of emerging trends is crucial for long-term competitiveness and operational efficiency. This chapter explores the role of automation and artificial intelligence (AI) in reshaping IT staffing, how remote work is transforming team structures, and the future skill sets IT professionals will need to thrive in an ever-changing technological environment.

7.1 The Rise of Automation and AI in IT Staffing

Automation and AI are rapidly reshaping the way organizations manage and deploy IT talent. These innovations streamline recruitment, task allocation, and project management, making the process of augmenting teams faster, more efficient, and increasingly precise. By integrating AI into staff augmentation, businesses can improve talent acquisition, enhance team performance, and boost productivity.

Strategic Approaches:

- AI-Powered Talent Acquisition: Traditional recruitment processes are often time-consuming and manual, but AI-powered platforms are revolutionizing the hiring process. These tools can scan thousands of resumes, analyze candidate skills, and match professionals to specific roles in a fraction of the time it takes human recruiters. Machine learning algorithms continuously refine the recruitment process, ensuring better candidate-job matching over time. Additionally, AI-driven chatbots and virtual assistants can provide an interactive candidate experience, speeding up the interview and onboarding stages.

  Example: A global retail corporation used an AI-driven recruitment tool to quickly source and onboard developers with expertise in cloud technologies for a critical system overhaul. The AI tool filtered through a high volume of candidates, identifying individuals with the specific technical expertise required, thus reducing recruitment time by over 40%.

- Automated Skill Matching and Optimization: After onboarding augmented staff, AI can play a key role in ensuring that team members are aligned with the most suitable tasks. By analyzing performance metrics and skill gaps, AI platforms can recommend changes in staffing allocations, ensuring that the team is optimized to deliver the best results.

  Example: A financial technology startup integrated AI into its project management platform to track the skill progress of augmented IT professionals. When performance data indicated a gap in cybersecurity expertise for an urgent project, AI automatically reassigned a specialist to fill the gap, optimizing the team's composition and accelerating project delivery.

- Robotic Process Automation (RPA) in IT Support: Routine tasks, such as system monitoring, ticketing management, and patch management, can be automated using RPA, freeing up augmented IT staff to focus on higher-value activities. RPA also ensures consistent execution of repetitive tasks, minimizing human error and increasing operational efficiency.

  Example: A leading e-commerce firm integrated RPA into its IT operations, automating routine tasks like database maintenance and software patch updates. This allowed their augmented developers to focus on strategic initiatives like enhancing the user experience, resulting in faster product releases and improved customer satisfaction.

Challenges from Client and Service Provider Perspectives:

From the client's perspective, the challenge lies in selecting the right AI and automation tools that integrate seamlessly with existing systems and processes. Companies must also balance the need for high-tech automation with the human element in team management.

From the service provider's side, the challenge is ensuring that augmented professionals are adequately trained to adapt to AI-powered tools and technologies, and that both the service provider and client have aligned expectations for performance optimization.

7.2 The Impact of Remote Work on IT Staff Augmentation

The increasing acceptance of remote work has dramatically shifted the IT staff augmentation model. With the help of communication and collaboration tools, businesses now have the flexibility to source IT talent from any location in the world. This global talent pool not only helps companies access specialized skills that may not be available locally, but also supports the growing trend of hybrid and distributed teams.

Strategic Approaches:

- Tapping into a Global Talent Pool: Remote work allows businesses to hire specialized professionals who may be in short supply in their local markets. Whether it's finding cloud engineers with expertise in AWS or Azure, AI and machine learning specialists, or developers experienced in emerging fields like blockchain, remote work allows companies to cast a wider net to find the best talent for their needs.

  Example: A tech company in the United States needed to scale up its team of blockchain developers quickly. By leveraging remote work, they were able to source top-tier blockchain experts from regions where expertise in smart contracts and decentralized technologies was more abundant, significantly accelerating their project timeline.

- Building Hybrid Teams: The rise of remote work enables businesses to create hybrid teams that combine in-house and augmented talent. This approach fosters diversity and brings in new perspectives, while simultaneously ensuring flexibility in staffing. However, managing these hybrid teams requires careful coordination to overcome challenges such as time zone differences and varied work cultures.

  Example: A multinational software company embraced hybrid staffing by integrating remote developers from South America with their core team in Europe. They leveraged cloud-based project management tools like Jira, Asana, and Slack to maintain seamless communication and coordinate tasks effectively, allowing the team to maintain high productivity despite geographical challenges.

- Time Zone Management and Flexibility: One of the biggest challenges with remote teams, especially those spread across different time zones, is managing coordination and communication. However, businesses can overcome these hurdles by adopting flexible work hours, utilizing asynchronous communication tools, and aligning core working hours for overlapping periods of collaboration.

  Example: A European digital marketing firm added remote staff from Asia to their team for a large project. By creating core working hours that overlapped between Europe and Asia, and using project management tools like Trello and Slack for asynchronous updates, the team was able to remain synchronized despite the time difference.

Challenges from Client and Service Provider Perspectives:

Clients often face difficulties in managing remote teams, particularly in coordinating workflows and ensuring consistent communication across various time zones. Remote work can also lead to challenges with building team cohesion and maintaining productivity without the structure of a physical office.

From the service provider's perspective, the challenge lies in maintaining visibility into team performance while managing cultural differences and ensuring that remote staff have access to the resources and support they need to thrive.

7.3 Future Skill Requirements for IT Professionals

As technology advances, the demand for IT professionals with specialized skill sets continues to grow. To stay competitive, businesses must ensure that their augmented teams are equipped with the necessary expertise in emerging technologies.

Strategic Approaches:

- AI and Machine Learning: As AI and machine learning become central to many industries, businesses need professionals skilled in data analysis, algorithm design, and predictive modeling. IT professionals with expertise in these fields will play a key role in shaping the future of automation, decision-making, and product innovation.
- Cloud Computing and DevOps: As companies move more of their operations to the cloud, the need for cloud engineers, DevOps professionals, and experts in containerization and cloud security is expected to grow. IT professionals with experience in cloud platforms like AWS, Azure, and Google Cloud,

as well as those versed in continuous integration/continuous deployment (CI/CD) practices, will be in high demand.

- Cybersecurity: With the increase in cyber threats and data breaches, businesses will continue to need IT professionals skilled in cybersecurity, including expertise in threat detection, ethical hacking, and compliance with privacy regulations. This skill set is critical in safeguarding company assets and customer data.
- Blockchain and Distributed Ledger Technologies: Blockchain has become a critical technology across various industries, including finance, healthcare, and logistics. Professionals with expertise in smart contracts, decentralized applications (dApps), and blockchain architecture will be sought after for developing secure, decentralized systems.
- Soft Skills and Adaptability: While technical expertise is crucial, the demand for soft skills such as creativity, problem-solving, and emotional intelligence will grow. As automation handles more routine tasks, IT professionals will need to demonstrate their ability to innovate, collaborate across functions, and adapt to rapidly changing technology landscapes.

Case Study:

A leading healthcare provider recognized the potential of blockchain to improve patient data security. To enhance their team's capabilities, they augmented their IT department with blockchain developers specializing in Ethereum and smart contracts. This move not only improved data privacy but also positioned the provider as a leader in secure healthcare technology.

7.4 Conclusion

The future of IT staff augmentation is shaped by the convergence of new technologies, shifting workforce models, and the growing need for specialized skills. Automation and AI are transforming how businesses recruit, manage, and optimize augmented teams, while remote work continues to expand the talent pool, offering new opportunities for collaboration. To remain competitive, businesses must adapt to the evolving skill requirements of the IT sector, focusing on emerging technologies like AI, cloud computing, cybersecurity, and blockchain.

By embracing these trends and aligning their staffing strategies accordingly, organizations can ensure they are well-prepared for the future—agile, innovative, and capable of addressing the challenges of an increasingly digital world. In the next chapter, we will delve into how businesses can maximize the return on investment (ROI) from their IT staff augmentation strategies, optimizing performance and sustaining long-term growth.

Chapter 8

Real-Life Case Studies and Success Stories in IT Staff Augmentation

In the fast-evolving world of IT, businesses are increasingly turning to staff augmentation as a strategic solution to address the growing complexity and diversity of technology needs. This model enables organizations to access specialized expertise, scale their teams swiftly, and meet critical project demands. However, the success of staff augmentation depends not only on selecting the right talent but also on integrating these professionals seamlessly into existing teams, ensuring alignment with company culture, and managing collaboration across different time zones and technological stacks.

In this chapter, we will explore a range of real-life case studies to uncover how businesses have effectively used

IT staff augmentation to their advantage, and examine lessons learned from instances where the model faced challenges. By analyzing both successful implementations and failures, organizations can draw key insights on how to optimize their own staff augmentation strategies, avoid common pitfalls, and achieve long-term success.

8.1 Successful Use Cases of IT Staff Augmentation

Staff augmentation has proven to be a game changer for many organizations across industries. Here are three real-world examples where IT staff augmentation enabled businesses to address critical technology gaps, accelerate product development, and streamline operations.

Case Study 1: Global E-commerce Platform's Mobile Expansion

- The Challenge:

  A leading global e-commerce company, primarily known for its online marketplace, sought to expand into mobile technology. While their internal IT team had extensive experience in web development, they lacked the expertise to develop a robust and scalable mobile application for both iOS and Android platforms. The project had tight deadlines, and the company needed skilled mobile developers to launch the app successfully in time for the holiday shopping season.

- The Solution:

  The company decided to augment its IT team with external mobile app developers who specialized in iOS and Android development. To ensure flexibility and expertise, they combined a mix of local and remote developers, leveraging their in-house team to provide domain-specific knowledge while the augmented team brought in the technical mobile experience.

- Implementation:

  The augmented team was quickly integrated into the company's Agile development process, participating in weekly sprints, code reviews, and planning meetings. Communication was streamlined using tools like Slack, Zoom, and Jira, enabling seamless collaboration despite geographical distances. By combining internal resources with augmented expertise, the company rapidly accelerated its mobile development timeline.

- Results:

  The mobile app was launched on schedule, and the company saw a 25% increase in mobile revenue within the first quarter. User reviews were overwhelmingly positive, highlighting the app's smooth user interface and robust functionality. The successful mobile launch demonstrated how augmenting the internal team with specialized expertise can accelerate innovation and product delivery.

Key Takeaways:

- Clear communication and defined roles are crucial for smooth integration of augmented staff.
- A hybrid team model that blends in-house and external talent fosters faster innovation.
- Staff augmentation allows for scalable resource allocation, ensuring optimal use of talent across fluctuating project phases.

Case Study 2: Cybersecurity Overhaul for a Global Financial Institution

- The Challenge:

  As cyber threats continued to increase in sophistication, a global financial institution recognized the urgent need to overhaul its cybersecurity infrastructure. The existing IT security team lacked the specialized knowledge in areas such as encryption, threat detection, and network security required to fortify their defenses against emerging risks and meet industry regulations.

- The Solution:

  The institution opted to augment their IT security team with highly experienced cybersecurity professionals who possessed deep expertise in network security and compliance. The augmented team was tasked with conducting a comprehensive audit and implementing advanced security measures across the institution's digital infrastructure.

- Implementation:

  The augmented team collaborated with the internal IT staff to develop and implement a security overhaul, using state-of-the-art cybersecurity tools and frameworks. They worked together to address vulnerabilities and ensure the system met compliance standards, including GDPR and SOC 2. The augmented team's expertise allowed the company to implement cutting-edge threat detection protocols and encryption technologies.

- Results:

  The cybersecurity overhaul was completed on time, and the organization successfully strengthened its defenses against cyber threats. As a result, the financial institution reported a 40% reduction in security breaches within the first six months, significantly improving its security posture and meeting regulatory deadlines.

Key Takeaways:

- Augmenting with specialized expertise allows businesses to address urgent needs quickly and effectively.

- A well-integrated augmented team can accelerate complex projects, such as security overhauls, that require deep technical knowledge.
- Staff augmentation allowed the institution to focus on core activities while strengthening its security capabilities.

Case Study 3: Cloud Migration for a Healthcare Provider

- The Challenge:

  A leading healthcare provider aimed to modernize its IT infrastructure by migrating legacy systems to the cloud. However, their internal team lacked the necessary expertise in cloud platforms such as AWS and Azure, as well as experience in executing large-scale migrations with minimal downtime. The transition was critical for improving operational efficiency and providing better patient care.

- The Solution:

  The company decided to augment its IT team with cloud engineers, architects, and DevOps professionals who had proven experience in large-scale cloud migrations. This expertise was crucial to ensuring the project met the healthcare provider's stringent security and compliance requirements.

- Implementation:

  The augmented team worked closely with the internal IT department to design a cloud migration strategy that minimized risks to patient data and ensured compliance with healthcare regulations. They leveraged best practices for cloud architecture, focusing on scalability, security, and availability. With a clear division of roles, the augmented team worked alongside internal IT to execute the migration seamlessly.

- Results:

  The migration was completed ahead of schedule, resulting in a 35% reduction in infrastructure costs within the first year. The cloud solution enabled the healthcare provider to scale its operations efficiently and improve service delivery, directly enhancing patient experience. The cloud infrastructure also provided better disaster recovery capabilities, which are critical in the healthcare sector.

Key Takeaways:

- Augmenting teams with cloud experts can fill critical gaps in knowledge, enabling successful migrations.
- Collaboration between internal and augmented staff is essential to ensure smooth transitions, especially in regulated industries.
- The flexibility to access on-demand cloud expertise allows businesses to mitigate risks and maximize ROI.

8.2 Lessons Learned from Challenges and Failures in IT Staff Augmentation

While IT staff augmentation can offer substantial benefits, not every attempt at augmenting teams results in success. Here are two cautionary tales that highlight the challenges of poorly executed augmentation strategies and offer valuable lessons for overcoming them.

Case Study 1: ERP System Overhaul in Retail

- The Challenge:

  A well-established retail company sought to overhaul its ERP system by augmenting its team with ERP specialists to integrate inventory, sales, and customer data. The goal was to streamline operations and improve business insights.

- The Issue:

  Despite bringing in technically proficient ERP consultants, the augmented team lacked a deep understanding of the company's unique business processes and culture. This gap led to misalignment between the augmented team's efforts and the company's internal workflows, resulting in frequent misunderstandings and delays.

- Results:

  The integration process faced multiple setbacks, causing the project to be delayed by several months.

Eventually, additional resources were required to resolve misalignments and bring the system live.

Key Takeaways:

- Cultural fit and alignment with internal processes are just as important as technical expertise.
- A comprehensive onboarding process is essential to help augmented teams understand internal workflows.
- Effective communication between augmented and internal teams is vital for smooth integration and project success.

Case Study 2: DevOps Implementation at a Software Firm

- The Challenge:

  A software company aimed to improve its software development lifecycle by implementing DevOps practices. They decided to augment their team with experienced DevOps engineers to help streamline development and deployment processes.

- The Issue:

  While the augmented DevOps engineers were technically skilled, they struggled to integrate with the existing development team. The firm underestimated the level of cultural change and internal resistance involved in adopting DevOps practices. The augmented team had difficulty adjusting to the internal team's existing workflows, causing friction and delayed progress.

- Results:

  The firm faced delays in fully adopting DevOps, as the augmented team was not adequately prepared for the cultural shift required. The full benefits of DevOps, including improved collaboration and faster deployments, were not realized.

Key Takeaways:

- Cultural alignment is essential for successful DevOps implementation.
- Augmented teams must undergo training and integration to align with internal processes and team dynamics.
- Clear alignment on goals, tools, and methodologies is crucial for DevOps success.

8.3 Conclusion

The case studies presented in this chapter illustrate the powerful impact that IT staff augmentation can have on organizations, enabling them to rapidly scale expertise, accelerate project timelines, and address critical skills gaps. However, success hinges on careful planning, clear communication, and strategic integration of external talent. Businesses that embrace a thoughtful, structured approach to staff augmentation can unlock its full potential, driving innovation and efficiency.

On the other hand, lessons from challenges and failures highlight the importance of aligning augmented teams with internal processes, fostering cultural integration, and managing expectations. By learning from both the successes and setbacks of others, organizations can refine their staff augmentation strategies, avoid common pitfalls, and stay ahead in a competitive digital landscape.

In the next chapter, we will explore strategies for optimizing the cost-effectiveness of IT staff augmentation, ensuring that businesses can achieve maximum return on investment while maintaining agility in an ever-changing technology landscape.

Chapter 9

Conclusion and the Path Forward

As we conclude this deep dive into IT staff augmentation, it is clear that this model has become a cornerstone strategy for organizations looking to stay ahead in today's fast-evolving digital world. The insights shared throughout this book underscore the versatility and power of staff augmentation as an approach to scaling operations, filling critical skill gaps, and driving innovation. However, just as it offers significant advantages, it also brings forth challenges that need to be navigated with a strategic mindset, clear communication, and a commitment to continuous improvement.

9.1 Recap of the Importance and Benefits of IT Staff Augmentation

In today's rapidly shifting technological landscape, IT staff augmentation offers businesses a flexible and scalable solution to meet their evolving needs. The growing demand for specialized expertise in areas like cloud computing, cybersecurity, artificial intelligence (AI), DevOps, and big data often outpaces the availability of skilled talent in the local workforce. IT staff augmentation allows companies to tap into a global talent pool, providing access to professionals with niche skills that may not be readily available in-house or within a specific geographic region.

The benefits of IT staff augmentation go beyond just filling skills gaps. Augmented teams allow businesses to scale operations quickly in response to fluctuating project demands, seasonal requirements, or sudden opportunities. This enables organizations to stay agile, minimize downtime, and meet critical deadlines without the cost and long-term commitment of traditional hiring processes.

For example, in the context of cloud migration, businesses can augment their teams with AWS, Azure, or Google Cloud Platform experts who bring the technical know-how needed to seamlessly transition from legacy infrastructure to modern cloud solutions. By integrating these specialists into existing teams, organizations can fast-track migrations, ensuring minimal disruption and greater scalability post-transition.

Furthermore, the ability to bring in cybersecurity professionals during high-risk periods, such as during the launch of a new digital product, enables businesses to bolster their defenses, implement advanced threat detection mechanisms, and address vulnerabilities before they become critical. Data scientists and machine learning engineers can be integrated into teams to assist with building advanced AI models, providing businesses with the data-driven insights they need to stay competitive.

By partnering with the right service providers, businesses can focus on their core competencies, knowing that specialized functions are being handled by experts. This can result in enhanced efficiency, reduced overhead, and a streamlined approach to project management and product delivery.

9.2 The Path Forward: A Call to Action for Businesses

Looking ahead, it is essential for businesses to understand that the future of IT staffing is dynamic and requires a forward-thinking approach. As new technologies and methodologies continue to reshape the business world, organizations that can quickly access specialized skills and adapt to changing needs will be the ones to succeed.

However, IT staff augmentation is not just about filling short-term gaps. To truly capitalize on its potential, businesses must approach this strategy with foresight and strategic intent. The success of staff augmentation lies in its integration within the organization's broader business objectives and technological infrastructure. Human Resource (HR) leaders must play a pivotal role in ensuring that augmented teams align with the organization's culture, values, and workflows.

From a client perspective, one of the key challenges is identifying the right mix of external talent and integrating it into existing teams. In some cases, the external team may lack an understanding of the company's business processes or organizational culture, leading to friction or delays. Clear communication, well-defined goals, and thorough onboarding processes are essential to overcoming this challenge. For instance, in DevOps adoption, augmented professionals must not only possess technical expertise but also understand the internal culture shift that DevOps entails. Without proper integration, the full benefits of agile development and continuous deployment may not be realized.

On the service provider side, the challenges often lie in delivering talent that not only meets the technical requirements but also fits seamlessly within the client's organizational framework. Providers must invest time in understanding the client's business model, communication protocols, and team dynamics. For example, a provider supplying cybersecurity experts must ensure that these professionals are well-versed in the client's specific security policies, risk profiles, and regulatory requirements.

Moreover, businesses must consider how to evaluate the effectiveness of their augmented teams. This is where the importance of Key Performance Indicators (KPIs) and service-level agreements (SLAs) cannot be overstated. Establishing clear expectations at the outset and measuring progress at regular intervals can ensure that external teams deliver on their promises and contribute to achieving business goals. This is especially important when augmenting teams in areas like AI development or big data analytics, where complex projects require precision and alignment with business outcomes.

As the demand for IT talent continues to grow, organizations must also be mindful of the cost implications of staff augmentation. While it offers many benefits, it is crucial to ensure that the investment in external talent provides a strong return on investment (ROI). Businesses must balance the cost of augmented resources with the value they bring to the project, ensuring that each engagement is cost-effective and aligns with long-term objectives.

9.3 Strategies for Successful IT Staff Augmentation

To successfully leverage IT staff augmentation, companies must adopt a structured approach. Key strategies for success include:

- Clear Goal Definition: Before engaging in staff augmentation, businesses must clearly define the goals and expectations of the project. This includes understanding the technological stack required (e.g., full-stack development, cloud infrastructure, cybersecurity frameworks) and the specific expertise needed (e.g., AWS Cloud Architect, Python Developer, DevOps Specialist).
- Thorough Talent Selection: Finding the right talent is critical. Businesses should partner with service providers who have a strong track record in delivering professionals who not only have the technical expertise but also understand the client's industry, challenges, and specific needs.
- Cultural and Process Integration: Ensuring that augmented staff are integrated into existing teams is vital. This includes providing onboarding that covers not only technical aspects but also company culture, workflow systems (e.g., Jira, Slack), and collaborative practices (e.g., Agile ceremonies, standups, and retrospectives).

- Regular Communication and Feedback: Maintaining open channels of communication between internal teams and augmented staff ensures that expectations are aligned, challenges are addressed quickly, and productivity remains high.
- Performance Measurement and Continuous Improvement: Establishing KPIs and regularly assessing the performance of augmented teams ensures that goals are being met and helps identify areas for improvement.

9.4 Conclusion: The Future of IT Staffing

As we look to the future, it's clear that businesses that effectively integrate IT staff augmentation into their long-term talent management strategies will have a distinct advantage in navigating the ever-evolving landscape of digital transformation. The pace of technological change shows no signs of slowing down, and organizations must remain agile, innovative, and resourceful to stay competitive. IT staff augmentation offers a powerful solution for businesses that want to maintain their ability to scale, access cutting-edge expertise, and continue driving innovation in a rapidly changing digital world.

The traditional approach of relying solely on in-house teams may no longer be sufficient to meet the increasingly specialized needs of today's technology landscape. From cloud computing and artificial intelligence (AI) to cybersecurity and big data analytics, the demands for specific technical skills have grown exponentially. The shortage of qualified professionals in these areas has made it increasingly difficult for organizations to find and retain the talent necessary to stay ahead. IT staff augmentation provides businesses with a flexible way to fill this gap, giving them access to specialized skill sets on-demand, without the lengthy hiring process or the overhead costs associated with permanent staffing.

However, businesses must approach IT staff augmentation with a strategic mindset, ensuring that it is not seen merely as a short-term solution to a specific project, but as an integral part of a long-term staffing strategy. The future of IT staffing lies in the ability to seamlessly blend internal talent with external expertise, creating dynamic teams that can respond quickly to market changes and technological advancements. This will require HR leaders to foster an environment where both internal employees and augmented staff work collaboratively toward shared goals, guided by a common vision.

One of the most important aspects of IT staff augmentation is that it offers businesses the flexibility to scale their teams based on evolving project needs. For example, in areas like DevOps or cloud migration, companies may need additional developers, systems engineers, or architects only for a defined period. With IT staff augmentation, they can onboard external talent to meet specific project requirements, reducing the risk of overstaffing or underutilizing resources. This ability to scale the team up or down is invaluable in today's fast-paced business environment, where companies must remain nimble to adapt to shifting priorities and deadlines.

However, this flexibility comes with its own set of challenges. Integrating augmented staff into existing teams can be difficult, especially when there are differences in working styles, communication approaches, or understanding of company culture. For IT staff augmentation to succeed, organizations must invest in proper onboarding, establish clear communication channels, and ensure that both internal and augmented teams are aligned on objectives, processes, and key performance indicators (KPIs). Misalignment in these areas can lead to inefficiencies, delays, and ultimately undermine the benefits of using external talent.

Moreover, for IT staff augmentation to truly work in the long term, businesses must also focus on creating a continuous learning culture. As new technologies emerge, the skill sets required to harness their full potential will change. Organizations need to stay proactive in their talent management strategies, ensuring that augmented staff have access to the training and resources they need to stay up-to-date with the latest developments in their field. At the same time, internal teams must also be given opportunities for growth and development to avoid skill gaps from emerging in the future. This commitment to continuous learning will not only ensure that organizations remain competitive but also foster an environment of innovation that can drive sustained growth.

From a human resources perspective, this approach requires a shift in how organizations think about talent. The traditional view of employees as permanent fixtures may need to evolve to accommodate a more fluid, hybrid workforce that includes both full-time staff and external experts. HR leaders will play a pivotal role in managing this transition, ensuring that the needs of both internal and augmented staff are met; and that collaboration between the two groups is seamless and productive. This includes managing expectations, fostering trust, and creating a work environment where everyone—whether internal or external—feels valued and integral to the organization's success.

Additionally, HR must lead the charge in creating an inclusive and collaborative workplace culture, even when teams are dispersed across different geographies. As remote work becomes more prevalent, it's essential for HR to implement tools, systems, and processes that promote effective communication, transparency, and cross-functional collaboration. Augmented teams, often working remotely or in different time zones, require strong coordination and the right digital tools to stay engaged and aligned with internal teams.

In terms of technology adoption, the future will bring even more opportunities for staff augmentation to be a key driver of innovation. Technologies such as blockchain, quantum computing, and edge computing are gaining traction, and businesses that are able to tap into augmented expertise in these fields will gain a significant competitive edge. However, success in these areas will require organizations to remain agile, continually assess their talent needs, and ensure that augmented staff have the skills required to implement and innovate with these new technologies.

Furthermore, the growing importance of data privacy and regulatory compliance will make cybersecurity and risk management even more critical. In this context, augmented IT teams, with their specialized expertise in areas such as network security, encryption, and compliance protocols, will be invaluable for organizations seeking to bolster their digital infrastructure. Having access to these experts on-demand will allow businesses to address vulnerabilities more quickly and effectively, ensuring that they remain secure and compliant in an increasingly complex regulatory environment.

In conclusion, the future of IT staffing is not just about filling roles or completing projects—it's about building a sustainable, dynamic workforce that is agile, innovative, and capable of meeting the ever-growing demands of digital transformation. IT staff augmentation offers a powerful solution for businesses looking to stay ahead of the curve, but only if it is approached with a strategic, long-term mindset. HR leaders must take the reins in ensuring that both internal teams and augmented staff are integrated effectively, aligned with the company's goals, and continuously developing their skills to keep pace with the changing technology landscape.

For businesses that embrace IT staff augmentation as a cornerstone of their talent strategy, the opportunities are vast. By leveraging the expertise of external professionals, businesses can drive innovation, accelerate growth, and ensure that they remain competitive in a fast-paced, digital-first world. The key to success lies in how effectively organizations manage these augmented teams, creating a collaborative, flexible, and continuous learning environment that allows them to adapt to both the challenges and opportunities that lie ahead.

Ultimately, the businesses that can successfully integrate external talent with internal teams, foster innovation, and maintain a strategic focus on long-term growth will be the ones that thrive in the digital age. The time to act is now.

Acknowledgments

This book would not have been possible without the incredible people who have supported, guided, and encouraged me throughout this journey.

To my family: Your unwavering love and belief in me have been the foundation of everything I've achieved. You have stood by me through every challenge, offering not just encouragement but also the practical and emotional support I needed to keep going. To my parents, thank you for instilling in me the values of hard work, resilience, and compassion. You taught me to dream big but always remain humble and grounded. To my bhai and bhabhi, thank you for your endless support, love, and encouragement. Your belief in my potential and your constant reminders to keep pushing forward have meant the world to me. The bond we share has been a source of strength and inspiration throughout this journey.

To my friends: Your encouragement, wisdom, and kindness have been invaluable. Thank you for being there to listen, offer advice, and remind me to take a break and laugh when things felt overwhelming.

To my colleagues: Collaborating with you has been a privilege. Your insights, teamwork, and passion have profoundly shaped my professional journey. Thank you for your trust and camaraderie.

To my mentor, Nimit Bheda: Your guidance has been a cornerstone of my growth and success. Professionally, you have been an inspiring leader, showing me how recruitment is not just about matching skills but about transforming businesses and empowering individuals. Your strategic vision and innovative approach to IT staff augmentation have deeply influenced my understanding of the industry. You taught me the importance of empathy, resilience, and long-term thinking in every decision I make.

On a personal level, your mentorship has been nothing short of life-changing. You saw potential in me when I doubted myself, pushing me to take on challenges I never thought I could handle. Your belief in my abilities gave me the confidence to pursue my passion with courage and conviction. Beyond your professional wisdom, your humility, patience, and unwavering support have been a constant source of inspiration.

Nimit, thank you for not only shaping my career but also for helping me grow as a person. Your influence goes far beyond professional guidance—it's a testament to the power of genuine mentorship. I am forever grateful for your trust, encouragement, and the profound impact you've had on my journey.

This book is as much a reflection of your contributions as it is of my own experiences. Thank you for being part of my story.

www.ingramcontent.com/pod-product-compliance
Lightning Source LLC
LaVergne TN
LVHW021159160826
845679LV00024B/2165

* 9 7 9 8 8 9 6 7 3 8 8 2 4 *